The Shepherd

For to us **a child is born,** to us a son is given; and the government shall be upon his shoulder, and his name shall be called WONDERFUL COUNSELOR, MIGHTY GOD, EVERLASTING FATHER, PRINCE OF PEACE.

Isaiah 9:6

By Dallas and Amanda Jenkins

Illustrated by Kristen Hendricks

BEAVER'S POND PRESS
SAINT PAUL

Written by Dallas and Amanda Jenkins
Illustration and design by Kristen Hendricks
Edited by Lily Coyle
File production by Dan Pitts

ISBN 13: 978-1-64343-747-7
Library of Congress Catalog Number: 2021911830
Printed in United States
First Printing: 2021
25 24 23 22 21   5 4 3 2 1

Beaver's Pond Press
939 Seventh Street West
Saint Paul, MN 55102
(952) 829-8818
www.BeaversPondPress.com

To order more of this book, visit: thechosen.tv/store

THESE ARE SHEPHERDS.

Many years ago, shepherds were dirty. And stinky. And poor.

WHICH MEANS THEY WERE LOWLY.

The job of the shepherds was to take care of
their sheep outside the city, where there were fields
for the flocks to walk and eat and sleep in.

Which is why the shepherds were stinky.
They worked and slept outside with the sheep.

Simon was a shepherd, so he was stinky and poor too.

AND HE HAD A HARD TIME WALKING BECAUSE
HIS LEG DIDN'T WORK RIGHT.

Which means Simon was the lowliest
of the lowly shepherds.

One day, the shepherds took their sheep into the city to sell in the marketplace.

But Simon's sheep had a spot on his leg, and no one wanted to buy him.

WHICH MEANS

Simon's sheep was the lowliest of all the sheep.

SO LOWLY SIMON AND HIS
LOWLY SHEEP WALKED BACK
TO THEIR LOWLY FIELD
OUTSIDE THE CITY.

BUT THAT NIGHT, SOMETHING

AMAZING

HAPPENED.

While the shepherds
kept watch over
their flocks by night,
suddenly the sky
was full of
bright lights and

ANGELS SAYING,

"Don't be afraid! We bring good news for all people! Today in the city of David, the Savior is born, who is Christ the Lord!"

Luke 2:10-11

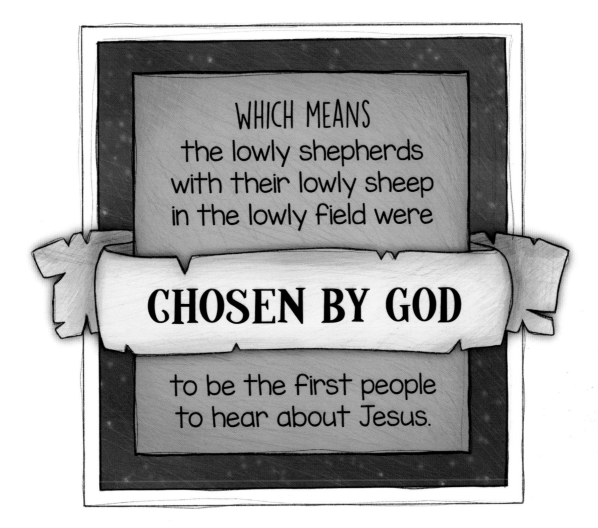

WHICH MEANS
the lowly shepherds
with their lowly sheep
in the lowly field were

CHOSEN BY GOD

to be the first people
to hear about Jesus.

Simon couldn't wait
to meet the One
the angels were proclaiming.

The One who would save the world

—including him—from sin and
sadness and loneliness and fear.

And because he was the lowliest shepherd in the lowliest field that night,

Simon got a head start when he ran to

Jesus.

Not even his leg could slow him down.

AND SUDDENLY, THERE IT WAS.

A LOWLY STABLE,
A QUIET LIGHT, AND A BABY.

The stable was stinky and the family inside it was poor.
They were lowly, like him.

But Simon knew he was kneeling in front of a King—
the angels told him so.

AND DEEP IN HIS HEART, HE COULD FEEL IT.

Jesus was the Savior

GOD'S
PEOPLE
HAD
BEEN
WAITING
FOR.

And the lowly shepherd with his lowly sheep from a lowly field was going to be the first person to tell others that

the Savior had come.

It didn't matter that Simon was a shepherd.
Or that he was poor. Or that his leg didn't work right.

Jesus

HAD COME TO
SAVE ALL PEOPLE,

including and
especially lowly
people. Which
includes us.

AND PEOPLE MUST KNOW.

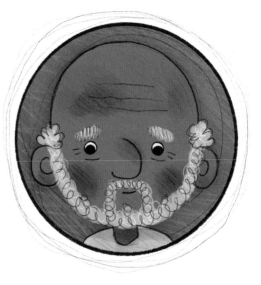